sasol
reaching new frontiers

FIRST FIELD GUIDE TO
COMMON
BIRDS
OF SOUTHERN AFRICA

D0180511

TRACEY HAWTHORNE

Contents

Page 36

Page 26

Southern African birds

Southern Africa is home to more than 900 different bird species. Not all of them are year-round residents, however – the 'jetsetters' of the bird world visit only for the summer or winter, flying north again when the season changes. Some Antarctic species visit southern Africa during the winter. Also, among our resident birds, quite a few are not easily seen – some are rare, and some prefer little-inhabited regions such as mountains and deserts, while others are nocturnal or very secretive.

Although only 46 species are covered in this book, many other southern African birds occur in large numbers in the region. Bear this in mind when you take this book with you on a bird-watching trip. The habitat map shown opposite will give you an idea of the different types of vegetation found in the region, while the regional map (opposite, bottom) shows the South African provinces, and should be used together with the distribution map shown alongside each species' account.

Page 13

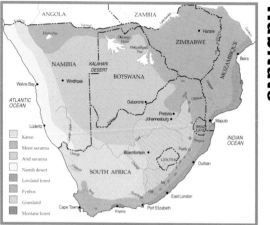

How to use this book

Page 10

Each species' account is split up into several headings, listed below.

Common name: The 'common name' is the English name by which the bird is known internationally. These have been updated in accordance with recommendations by an international committee.

Scientific name: This is the official name by which the bird is known throughout the world, and is always written in *italic* type.

African names: The bird's name in Afrikaans (**A**), Xhosa (**X**) and Zulu (**Z**) – the most commonly spoken South African languages after English – where available.

Average size: The total **length** of the bird is given. This is measured from bill tip to tail tip with the bird stretched out, so it will be slightly longer than the bird's measurement as seen in the field. Use the ruler on the outside back cover for a realistic idea of how big the bird is.

The **wingspan** (the measurement from wingtip to wingtip) is given where this information is available; otherwise, the measurement of a single **wing**, from 'elbow' to wingtip, is provided. Only where male and female measurements differ significantly are both given.

Identification: The colours of the bird's plumage and bare parts, as well as other physical charac-teristics that will help you to identify the bird.

Call: Difficult to put into words, this is intended only as a rough guide to the sound the bird makes.

Where found: What environment the bird prefers. This, together with the distribution map that accompanies the species' account, will tell you where a specific bird is likely to be seen. The southern African region includes South Africa, Lesotho, Swaziland, Namibia, Botswana, Zimbabwe and Mozambique.

Habits: The bird's behaviour (for instance, whether it is gregarious^G or solitary^G) and its feeding habits.

Nesting: The time of year a bird breeds, the type of nest it builds, the number and appearance of the eggs it lays, and the incubation^G period of its eggs.

Where relevant, the bird's breeding behaviour is also described.

Notes: Anything of special significance or interest.

Status: Most of the birds in this book are common residents, which means that they occur throughout the year in the region.

Similar species: Bear in mind that in many cases similar-looking species do not necessarily occur in the same location or habitat as the birds discussed in this book.

Food: What food the bird prefers.

A small, uppercase ^G *after a word indicates that it is explained in the* Glossary *on page 56.*

Page 22

Being a bird-watcher

Some people become a little intimidated when setting out to watch birds for the first time – after all, there are so many of them, and they all look so similar!

With a little practice, though, you will soon be able to identify one or two species, and soon this number will grow to 10 or 12, and before you know it you will be a fully fledged 'twitcher' (this is the name given to fanatical bird-watchers who try to identify as many different species as possible).

What bird is it?

The first step in identifying a bird, aside from obvious things like its size, colour and where you have spotted it, is its 'jizz', which means its overall look and behaviour. If, for instance, it hops energetically about on the ground, it could be a sparrow; but if it is walking slowly along like a stately old man, it might be an ibis.

Bear in mind when reading this book that a 'small' vulture will obviously be much bigger than a 'small' dove. The length of the bird

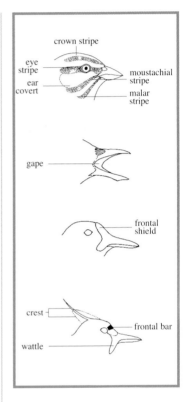

(given in centimetres) and the ruler on the outside back cover will help you to compare the size of the bird you have spotted in the field, with the species featured in this book.

Check these things to identify a bird

↓ What **size** is the bird you see?

↓ Study the **shape** of the bird, paying particular attention to its body, head, bill and tail shapes.

↓ Male birds are particularly colourful. Try to identify the **colours** of different body, plumage and bare parts (the parts of the bird are shown left and right).

↓ What is the bird doing, and is its **behaviour** normal?

↓ Where is the bird **feeding** or **nesting?**

↓ The distribution map will show you if the species you have spotted is found in your **region**.

Bird names

All birds have a local common name (for example, Grey Lourie), a scientific name (*Corythaixoides concolor*), and, sometimes, one or more alternative names (for example, Go-away Bird).

Be Aware!

Don't disturb birds, particularly if they are breeding. Never touch their nests, eggs or chicks – the parents might desert their young if you have interfered with them. Watch from a distance, through binoculars if you have them.

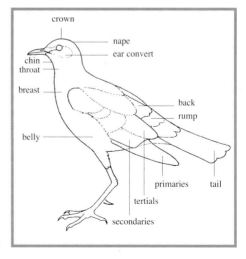

Jackass Penguin

Spheniscus demersus

African names: Brilpikkewyn (A); inguza, unombombiya (X).

Average size: Length 60 cm; length of flipper 16,5 cm.

Identification: A flightless bird whose wings are mere 'flippers'. Black chin and face patch, separated from crown by broad white band; narrow black band across chest and down flanks. Pink skin above eye.

Call: Loud, donkey-like braying at night; also honks and growls.

Where found: Offshore islands and at sea; less often on mainland.

Habits: Lives in small groups on the coast or in huge groups on offshore islands. Forages underwater at sea, coming to land to roost^G and breed.

Nesting: Year round, mainly in summer. Breeds colonially^G on

offshore islands. One or two white eggs are laid in a hollow dug into guano^G or sandy ground. These take five to six weeks to hatch.

Notes: Collection and selling of eggs, guano^G scraping, overfishing and oil spills have contributed to the decrease in its numbers.

Status: Resident endemic^G. 'Vulnerable'.

Food: Fish, squid.

Little Grebe

Tachybaptus ruficollis

African names:
Kleindobbertjie (A);
unolwilwilwi,
unoyamembi (X).

Average size: Length 20 cm;
wing 9-10 cm.

Identification: Blackish above,
pale rufous[G] below. Creamy-
white spot at base of bill, most
conspicuous in breeding season.
White secondaries visible in flight.

Call: Noisy: shrill, whinnying trill
and loud, sharp 'chik' alarm note.

Where found: Throughout, but
rare in desert areas; usually in
well-vegetated, still or slow-
flowing freshwater areas.

Habits: Often runs pattering
across surface of water with
wings flapping.

Nesting: Breeds year round,
mainly in spring and summer.
Builds a floating heap of water
plants low in the water, in which
two to five white or bluish eggs
are laid. These eggs hatch after
about three weeks.

Notes: Small chicks are sometimes
carried on the adult's back.

Status: Common resident.

Food: Small aquatic animals
(frogs, tadpoles, fish, etc.).

Similar species: Non-breeding
Blacknecked Grebe has white
cheeks and throat; when breeding,
lacks the creamy spot at the base
of the bill.

Eastern White Pelican

Pelecanus onocrotalus

African names:
Witpelikaan (A);
ingcwanguba (X);
ivubu, ifuba (Z).

Average size: Length 140-180 cm;
wingspan 272-305 cm (m),
226-266 cm (f).

Identification: Adult is very
large, mostly white, tinged with
pink when breeding. Pink bill
with yellowish pouch; pink legs.
Wings black and white in flight.
Immature^G is browner, but lightens
in colour with age.

Call: Usually silent; may grunt
or moo in breeding colonies.

Where found: Low-lying areas of
the west and east, on open water
bodies, coastal bays and estuaries.

Habits: Usually gregarious^G.
Forages in coordinated groups,
forming a 'net' around fish.

Nesting: Year round. Nests in
colonies of thousands. Up to
three eggs are laid and hatch
after six weeks. Both sexes
incubate^G and feed young.

Notes: Can swallow
fish weighing up
to 4 kg.

Status: Locally common
resident.

Food: Fish, but they
also scavenge.

Similar species:
Pinkbacked Pelican is
smaller and greyer.

Cape Gannet

Morus capensis

African names: Witmalgas (A); umkholonjane (X).

Average size: Length 84-94 cm; wingspan 171-185 cm; wing 45-51 cm.

Identification: Body mainly white, with straw-yellow head. Cobalt-blue ring around the eye; heavy, long, pointed, pale blue-grey bill; long black line down centre of throat; black, pointed tail.

Call: Raucous, rasping calls when feeding and at breeding colonies.

Where found: Along entire coast; offshore coastal waters.

Habits: These gregarious[G], aggressive birds may plunge-dive for fish from considerable heights. They are known for their 'sky-pointing' displays[G].

Nesting: Mainly in summer. Monogamous[G]. Nest is a guano[G] platform with a hollow top, in which one bluish-white egg is laid. Incubation[G], by both sexes, is done with webs of feet. The egg hatches after about six weeks.

Notes: Hundreds of these birds follow the 'sardine run' up the KwaZulu-Natal coast each winter.

Status: Common resident; breeding endemic[G].

Food: Fish.

Similar species: None.

Cape Cormorant

Phalacrocorax capensis

African names: Trekduiker (A); ugwidi (X).

Average size: Length 61-65 cm; wingspan 109 cm.

Identification: Mainly glossy blue-black; yellow throat; turquoise eye.

Call: Usually silent; clucks and croaks at breeding colonies.

Where found: Coastal waters along the entire coast.

Habits: Highly gregarious[G]; it flies in long lines over the sea before settling in large flocks to feed by diving from the surface. Aggressive when breeding.

Nesting: Breeds in dense colonies year round, but mainly in spring, and usually on islands. Nest is a shallow bowl of sticks, in which up to five pale, blue-green eggs are laid, which hatch after about three weeks. Both sexes incubate[G].

Notes: These birds provide a valuable annual harvest of guano[G], particularly off the coast of Namibia.

Status: Resident; breeding endemic[G].

Food: Fish, crustaceans.

Similar species: Bank Cormorant lacks yellow facial skin.

African Darter

Anhinga rufa

African names: Afrikaanse Slanghalsvoël (A); ivuzi (X).

Average size: Length 80 cm; wing 33-36 cm.

Identification: Dark above, rufous[G] below, with white streaks on wings. Long, kinked neck; long tail and straight, pointed bill.

Call: Usually silent; croaks harshly on nest.

Where found: Widespread on inland waters, estuaries and lagoons.

Habits: Swims low in the water. Dives well and spears fish underwater with bill. Roosts[G] communally.

Nesting: Year-round. Builds platform of sticks and reeds in which two to seven greenish or bluish eggs are laid. These hatch after three to four weeks. Both parents incubate[G] and feed young.

Notes: Darters are sometimes called 'Snakebirds' because of their habit of swimming with their entire body submerged, with only the head and neck showing above the water. Often seen sitting with their wings outspread, a habit they share with cormorants.

Status: Common resident.

Food: Fish, frogs, arthropods.

Similar species: Cormorants lack the rufous[G]-coloured, kinked neck, and have hooked bills.

Little Egret

Egretta garzetta

African names: Kleinwitreier (A); ingekle (Z).

Average size: Length 65 cm; wing 24-30 cm.

Identification: All-white plumage. Black bill and legs; yellow feet.

Call: Gargling, chattering and harsh, heron-like croak at take-off.

Where found: Virtually throughout; always near water.

Habits: Usually solitary^G when feeding but roosts^G in groups. When feeding, may disturb bottom-dwelling prey by shuffling foot in pool bottom.

Nesting: Mainly in summer. Nests colonially^G, building platform of sticks in which two to four pale greenish-blue eggs are laid. These hatch after about three weeks. Both sexes incubate^G and feed young.

Notes: This bird was once hunted extensively for its plumes, called 'aigrettes', which were used to adorn dresses and hats.

Status: Common resident.

Food: Fish, frogs, insects.

Similar species: Great White Egret is larger and has black feet; Yellowbilled Egret has yellow bill; Cattle Egret has short yellow bill.

Hamerkop

Scopus umbretta

African names:
Hamerkop (A);
uthekwane,
uqhimngqoshe (X);
uthekwane (Z).

Average size: Length 56 cm;
wingspan 90-94 cm.

Identification: Plain dark
brown. Large bill and heavy
crest giving 'hammerhead'
appearance.

Call: Noisy yelping and
squawking.

Where found: Virtually
throughout; most common in
east. Occurs on inland waters
(dams, lakes, rivers).

Habits: Usually solitary^G or in
small groups. Wades about in
shallow water in search of food,
occasionally stirring pool bottom
with foot.

Nesting: Year round, mainly in
spring. Builds huge, oven-shaped
nest of sticks, reeds and debris
(sometimes cooperatively with
up to four other birds) with a
small side entrance. Lays up
to five white eggs which hatch
after about a month. Both
sexes incubate^G.

Notes: The nest can take up to
six months to build and measure
up to two metres in diameter; it
is so strong that a man can stand
on its roof. It is often taken over
by other birds or bees.

Status: Common resident.

Food: Frogs, fish.

Similar species: None.

African Sacred Ibis

Threskiornis aethiopicus

African names: Skoorsteenveër (A); umxwagele (Z).

Average size: Length 90 cm; wing 38 cm.

Identification: Large. Mostly white plumage. Naked black head and neck; long, black bill curves downward. In flight, wings are white with black tips and trailing edges.

Call: Usually silent; croaks and squeals in breeding colonies.

Where found: Varied: inland waters, cultivated lands, sewage works and rubbish dumps, and coastal lagoons. Mainly in southern and eastern regions.

Habits: Gregarious[G], with flocks sometimes numbering in hundreds. Feeds on ground; scavenges in farming areas. Roosts[G] in trees, reedbeds or on islands.

Nesting: Spring and summer. In courtship, may inflate neck like a balloon. Nests colonially[G], building stick platforms. Lays two to five eggs which hatch after about a month. Both sexes incubate[G] and feed young.

Notes: This bird was once revered in Ancient Egypt.

Status: Common resident.

Food: Varied: arthropods, small mammals, nestling birds, eggs, small reptiles, carrion, seeds.

Similar species: None.

Greater Flamingo

Phoenicopterus ruber

African names: Grootflamink (A); ukholwase, unondwebu (Z).

Average size: Length 127-140 cm; wing 40-46 cm (m), 36-39 cm (f).

Identification: Large, with a long neck and long legs. Generally pale pink to white. Pink bill with black tip, bent in middle; pink legs. Bright-red forewing seen in flight.

Call: Gooselike honking.

Where found: Patchily throughout, on freshwater lakes, salt pans, estuaries, coastal lagoons.

Habits: Highly gregarious[G], flocks often numbering in thousands. Feeds by wading with bill upside-down in water, sifting through mud. Swims in deeper water.

Nesting: After summer rains. Nests in dense colonies. Mud nest is volcano-shaped. One pale

blue egg is laid and is incubated[G] for about a month by both parents.

Status: Common but nomadic resident.

Food: Aquatic insects, crustaceans, molluscs, microscopic algae.

Similar species: Lesser Flamingo is smaller and redder overall, and has a dark red bill.

Blue Crane

Anthropoides paradiseus

African names:
Bloukraanvoël (A);
indwe (X);
indwa (Z)

Average size: Length 100-107 cm;
wing 51-59 cm.

Identification: Blue-grey, with
long, slate-grey feathers curving
to the ground like tail streamers.
White crown.

Call: Noisy; high-pitched, guttural,
rattling 'kraaank'.

Where found: Vlei edges,
grassland and agricultural lands in
southern and eastern South Africa,
and at Etosha Pan in Namibia.

Habits: In pairs or family groups
when breeding, otherwise highly
gregarious[G]. Roosts[G] in flocks.

Nesting: Display[G] dances
performed in pairs or groups. In
summer, lays one to three pinkish-
brown eggs on bare ground,
sometimes surrounding eggs with
bits of grass or pebbles. The eggs
hatch after about a month.

Notes: South Africa's national
bird.

Status: Fairly common resident;
endemic[G].

Food: Frogs, insects, reptiles, fish,
grain, grass.

Similar species: Grey-coloured
herons lack the long tertial plumes.

Red-knobbed Coot

Fulica cristata

African names: Bleshoender (A); unomkqayi, unompemvana (X).

Average size: Length 44 cm; wingspan 75-85 cm.

Identification: All black, with white bill and frontal shield backed by two dark red knobs, which swell and become more visible during breeding season.

Call: Resonant clucking; snorting alarm call.

Where found: Virtually throughout, on inland waters, sometimes slow-flowing rivers, coastal lagoons.

Habits: Usually in pairs or large flocks; gregarious[G] when not breeding. Swims about on open water; forages by diving and grazing along the shoreline. Can fly long distances.

Nesting: Breeds year round, making nest of large heap of water plants in open water. Lays three to nine eggs, which hatch after about three weeks. Both sexes care for chicks, sometimes dividing the brood between them.

Notes: Toes are lobed, not webbed as in ducks.

Status: Common to abundant resident.

Food: Water plants, seeds, aquatic insects.

Similar species: Common Moorhen has a red frontal shield and yellow bill tip.

Egyptian Goose

Alopochen aegyptiaca

African names: Kolgans (A); ilowe (X); ilongwe (Z).

Average size: Length 63-73 cm; wing 34-41 cm.

Identification: Mainly buff-brown above. Dark brown eye mask; dark brown patch on centre of breast. Metallic-green secondaries. In flight shows conspicuous white forewings.

Call: Hissing (male only) and honking; calls with neck outstretched.

Where found: Throughout the region, except in deserts. Occurs on inland waters, estuaries and coastal lakes, and in cultivated fields.

Habits: Gregarious^G when not breeding, otherwise in pairs. Wary, quickly flies off when approached.

Nesting: Monogamous^G. Breeds year round, mainly in spring. Lays five to 11 cream-coloured eggs, which hatch after about a month. Female incubates^G; both parents feed young.

Notes: This bird was considered sacred by the Ancient Egyptians. It is valued as a gamebird. Can become an agricultural pest.

Status: Very common resident.

Food: Grass, leaves, seeds, grain, aquatic rhizomes and tubers.

Similar species: South African Shelduck lacks brown eye mask and breast patch.

African Fish Eagle

Haliaeetus vocifer

African names:
Visarend (A);
unomakhwezana (X);
inkwazi (Z).

Average size: Length 63-73 cm;
wingspan 191 cm (m), 237 cm (f).

Identification: Dark body and
wings; white head, nape and
breast. Short, square, white tail.
Dark chestnut belly and forewings.
Female is larger.

Call: Unmistakable, ringing
'kyow-kyow-kow'.

Where found: Mainly in north,
east and south on large water
bodies, lagoons and estuaries.

Habits: Usually in pairs. Hunts
from a perch, stooping^G at fish and
catching them in its claws. Steals
food from other birds, raids
waterbird colonies and scavenges.

Nesting: Mainly in winter.
Builds large stick nest, in which
up to three white eggs are laid.

These hatch after about six weeks.
Both sexes incubate^G; nestlings
fed mostly by female.

Notes: Very vocal; one of the best-
known and most studied birds.

Status: Locally common resident.

Food: Fish, carrion, nestlings
and eggs, small mammals, lizards,
frogs, insects.

Similar species: Palmnut Vulture
has extensive white in the wing
and a bare facial patch around
the eye.

Black-shouldered Kite

Elanus caeruleus

African names: Blouvalk (A); umdlampuku, unongwevana (X).

Average size: Length 33 cm; wingspan 74 cm.

Identification: Pale grey above, white below. Diagnostic[G] black shoulder patches. Black bill with yellow cere; yellow feet; red eye.

Call: Wheezy 'peeu' whistles and screams; soft 'weeep-weeep'.

Where found: Virtually through-out, in varied habitats (agricultural areas; also grassland, woodland, savannah, semi-arid scrub).

Habits: Solitary[G] or in pairs by day; roosts[G] communally at night. Hunts from perch or by hovering over prey.

Nesting: Year round, mainly in rainy seasons; may breed several times a year. Both sexes build a small, stick platform in which two to six eggs are laid. Incubation[G], mostly by female, takes a month.

Notes: Very common; often seen perched on telephone poles.

Status: Common resident with local movements.

Food: Mainly rodents; also small birds, reptiles and insects.

Similar species: Lizard Buzzard has black streak down throat and two broad, white tail bands.

White-backed Vulture

Gyps africanus

African name: Witrugaasvoël (A).

Average size: Length 90-98 cm; wingspan 212-228 cm.

Identification: Large. Generally streaky brown. Blackish face and neck. White lower back in flight. Dark eyes.

Call: Goose-like hisses, cackles and squeals; grunts.

Where found: Northern half of region, in savannah and bushveld.

Habits: Gregarious^G. Roosts^G in trees at night; often rests on ground during day. Drinks and bathes regularly at waterholes.

Nesting: In winter. Builds platform of sticks high in a tree; may use nest for a few years. One white egg is laid. Both sexes incubate^G; egg hatches after about two months. Both sexes feed young.

Notes: The most common vulture in southern Africa, and the most frequently seen in bushveld game reserves.

Status: Locally common resident.

Food: Carrion (softer parts of large game mammals), bone fragments.

Similar species: Cape Vulture is larger and paler, has yellow eyes and lacks white back.

Ostrich

Struthio camelus

African names:
Volstruis (A);
inciniba (X);
intshe (Z).

Height: Male up to 2 m.

Identification: Very large. Long, grey, bristly neck; long legs. Male mostly black, with mostly white wings and white, buff or rufous[G] tail. Female brownish-grey.

Call: Deep, booming, lion-like roar, made at night.

Where found: Virtually throughout, in bushveld to desert.

Habits: Sociable, often seen in groups of up to 10 birds. Forages among short vegetation.

Nesting: Year round. Males perform elaborate courtship displays[G] in breeding season. Nest is scrape in sandy soil in which up to 43 eggs are laid by several females. These hatch after six to seven weeks.

Notes: The largest flightless bird in the world. Can run at speeds of up to 60 km/h. The only wild ostriches are in Namibia and the Kalahari. Ostriches are farmed for their feathers, skin, eggs and flesh.

Status: Resident.

Food: Mainly herbivorous (grass, berries, seeds, succulent plants); sometimes small reptiles, insects.

Similar species: None.

Common Moorhen

Gallinula chloropus

African name: Grootwater-hoender (A).

Average size: Length 30-36 cm; wingspan 45 cm.

Identification: Dull, sooty black except for white undertail and white streaks on flanks. Red eye; red bill with yellow tip; red frontal shield.

Call: Sharp, nasal 'kirrik' or 'kik-kik-kik'; murmuring 'kook'.

Where found: Practically throughout, on virtually any fresh water surrounded by reeds and tall grasses.

Habits: Solitary[G] or in small family groups. Flicks tail when alarmed. Flies heavily with legs dangling.

Nesting: Year round; may raise up to eight broods a year. Territorial[G] when breeding. Both sexes build bowl of rushes and reeds above

water level. Lays four to nine eggs, which hatch after about three weeks. Female incubates[G] during the day, male by day and night.

Notes: One of the most widely distributed birds in the world.

Status: Common resident.

Food: Mainly vegetable matter (waterplants, seeds, berries); also molluscs, worms, spiders, insects, tadpoles.

Similar species: Lesser Moorhen is smaller and bill is mainly yellow; Lesser Gallinule has more colourful plumage and lacks white on flanks.

Helmeted Guineafowl

Numida meleagris

African names:
Gewone Tarentaal
(A); impangele (X);
impangele (Z).

Average size: Length 53-58 cm;
wing 24-29 cm.

Identification: Slate-grey body
finely spotted with white. Small,
naked, blue-and-red head.
Prominent 'helmet'.

Call: Grating 'cherrrrr' or
staccato 'kek-kek-kek' alarm
call; also whistles.

Where found: Virtually throughout, in grassland, vleis, savannah,
cultivated lands, bushveld.

Habits: Gregarious^G; flocks
may number in hundreds. Roosts^G
communally in trees at night.

Nesting: Mainly in summer, in
long grass or under bush. Six to
19 light yellowish-brown eggs
are laid. They hatch after about
a month. Only female incubates^G.

Notes: More than one female may
lay eggs in the same nest,
producing a combined clutch
of up to 50 eggs.

Status: Common resident.

Food: Seeds, bulbs, tubers, berries,
insects, snails, ticks.

Similar species: Crested Guinea-
fowl has black head plumes.

Blacksmith Lapwing (Plover)

Vanellus armatus

African names:
Bontkiewiet (A);
indudumela (Z).

Average size: Length 30 cm;
wing 20-22 cm.

Identification: Bold black, white
and grey coloration. Grey wings;
black nape, face, back and breast;
white forehead, crown and belly.
Ruby-red eye.

Call: Piercing 'klink-klink-klink'.

Where found: Throughout, on
shorelines of dams and sewage
ponds, playing fields, tidal flats in
bays and lagoons.

Habits: Solitary[G] or in pairs; non-
breeders gather in flocks. Wary by
nature, but aggressive in defence
of their nest.

Nesting: Year round. Nest is a
scrape on open ground, often
near water. Two to four well-
patterned eggs are laid; these
hatch after about a month. Both
sexes incubate[G].

Notes: Its call, which sounds like a
hammer on an anvil, gave rise to
its common name.

Status: Common resident.

Food: Insects, spiders, worms,
small molluscs.

Similar species: Longtoed Plover
has white face and foreneck.

Crowned Lapwing (Plover)

Vanellus coronatus

African names: Kroonkiewiet (A); igxiya (X).

Average size: Length 30 cm; wing 19-22 cm.

Identification: Mainly greyish-brown; dark band separating brown breast from white belly. Black crown, ringed with white 'halo'; black forehead. Long red legs.

Call: Very noisy: strident 'kreeep'.

Where found: Virtually throughout, in short grasslands and other lawn-like habitats.

Habits: Gregarious[G] when not breeding. Often active at night.

Nesting: Mostly in spring. Two to four well-marked, dark olive-brown eggs are laid in shallow scrape in ground. Both sexes incubate[G]; eggs hatch after about a month.

Notes: Quick to react to disturbance, will scream at intruders; birds with young or hatching eggs will noisily 'divebomb' intruders.

Status: Common resident.

Food: Arthropods.

Similar species: No other similarly sized plover has a white halo and a black crown.

Kelp Gull

Larus dominicanus

African names: Swartrugmeeu (A); ingaba-ngaba (X).

Average size: Length 50-60 cm; wingspan 127-132 cm.

Identification: Large. Mostly white, with black back and wings. Heavy yellow bill with red spot near tip; olive legs.

Call: Loud 'kee-ow'; mewing; screams in defence at nest.

Where found: Along entire coast; most abundant on west coast. Common in estuaries, beaches, harbours and rubbish dumps.

Habits: Forages by walking or flying. Follows ships for scraps and scavenges at harbours. Pilfers nests of other seabirds, taking eggs and small young. Steals food from other seabirds.

Nesting: Mainly in summer. Nest is a scrape on the ground, in which up to three pale green-, blue- or ochre-splotched eggs are laid. These hatch after about a month. Both sexes incubate[G].

Status: Common to abundant resident.

Food: Fish, offal, invertebrates, birds' eggs and young birds.

Similar species: Lesser Blackbacked Gull is smaller and has yellow legs.

Speckled Pigeon

Columba guinea

African names: Kransduif (A); ivukuthu (X); ijub, ivukuthu (Z).

Average size: Length 33 cm; wing 22-24 cm.

Identification: Large pigeon with mostly grey head and underparts; bare red patch around eye. Reddish-brown wings are conspicuously spotted with white. Black bill.

Call: Deep 'hooo-hooo-hooo' and mellow cooing.

Where found: Virtually throughout, on mountains, cliffs and in urban areas.

Habits: Solitary[G] or gregarious[G]. Feeds by day in agricultural lands.

Nesting: Year round. Nest is platform of sticks and grass built on a ledge, rarely in trees. The two white eggs hatch after about two weeks. Both parents incubate[G] and feed young.

Notes: Sometimes hybridises[G] with Feral Pigeons.

Status: Common resident.

Food: Seeds, fallen grain, green shoots.

Similar species: Feral Pigeon lacks white-spotted wings; Rameron Pigeon is larger, darker and has yellow legs, eye patch and bill.

Laughing Dove

Streptopelia senegalensis

African names:
Rooiborsduifie (A);
uvelemaxhoseni (X);
ukhonzane (Z).

Average size: Length 26 cm;
wing 13-15 cm.

Identification: Small; deep-rufous^G chest spotted with
black. Pinkish-grey head.
Cinnamon back.

Call: Bubbling cooing, rising
then falling.

Where found: A wide range of
habitats, but avoids forests.

Habits: Like other
doves, depends on
surface water and
drinks daily.

Nesting: Year round,
mainly in dry season.
Up to four white
eggs are laid; these
hatch after about two
weeks. Both parents

incubate^G and feed young;
'pigeon's milk' (regurgitated
from the crop) is fed to hatchlings.

Notes: Probably the best-known
of all our doves, it is found all
over and has adapted well to
cities and gardens. Its
common name derives from
its laughing call.

Status: Abundant resident.

Food: Seeds, grain, termite
alates, insects and larvae, snails.

Similar species: Cape Turtle
Dove has black hind collar.

Grey Go-away-bird (Lourie)

Corythaixoides concolor

African names: Kwêvoël (A); umklewu (Z).

Average size: Length 47-50 cm; wing 21-23 cm.

Identification: Large. Plain ash-grey all over, with long, shaggy head crest and long tail. Black bill, legs and feet.

Call: Nasal 'g'way' or 'kweh-h-h'; also grunts and shrieks.

Where found: In north of region, in bushveld, savannah, riverine woodland and arid country; also suburban gardens.

Habits: In pairs or small groups. Quick and agile in trees, but with a laboured flight. Highly vocal, especially when disturbed. Raises and lowers crest when alarmed.

Nesting: Year round. Builds platform of sticks in a tree, in which it lays two or three pale bluish-white eggs. These take about four weeks to hatch. Both sexes incubate[G] and feed young by regurgitation.

Notes: This is sometimes known as the 'Go-away Bird' on account of its call.

Status: Common resident.

Food: Fruit, flowers, buds, leaves, seeds.

Similar species: None.

Spotted Eagle Owl

Bubo africanus

African names: Gevlekte Ooruil (A); ifubesi (X); isikhovampondo (Z).

Average size: Length 43-50 cm; wing 32-37 cm.

Identification: Large. Grey above, sparsely spotted with white; finely barred dark grey below. Brown spots on breast. Yellow eyes. Very noticeable 'ear tufts'.

Call: Soft, hooting 'hu-hoo'; hissing in defence.

Where found: Throughout, in rocky areas, woodland, savannah and gardens.

Habits: Solitary^G or in pairs. Nocturnal, roosting^G by day and hunting by night.

Nesting: Mostly winter and spring. Usually lays two white eggs in a scrape. Eggs hatch after about a month. Female incubates^G.

Notes: Most common large owl in the region. Rare rufous^G colour form occurs, closely resembling Cape Eagle Owl.

Status: Common resident.

Food: Arthropods, birds, reptiles, small mammals, frogs.

Similar species: Cape Eagle Owl is heavily blotched, not barred, below, and has orange eyes.

Barn Owl

Tyto alba

African names: Nonnetjie-uil (A); isikhova (X, Z).

Average size: Length 30-34 cm; wing 24-30 cm.

Identification: Pale tawny and grey above, with small white spots; whitish underparts, with fine brown spots from breast to belly. White, heart-shaped face with small, dark eyes.

Call: Eerie, screeching 'schreee'; hissing in defence.

Where found: Throughout, in woodland to desert; avoids forest.

Habits: Usually in pairs. Roosts^G by day in suitable cavity, often in buildings. Weaves head from side to side in threat display^G.

Nesting: Throughout year (varies regionally). Two to 13 white eggs are laid, over intervals of up to three days, on flat floor of suitable cavity. They hatch after about a month. Female incubates^G. Nest may contain range of growing young, from newly hatched to fully feathered birds.

Notes: Found almost worldwide, often in buildings, which gives rise to its common name.

Status: Common resident.

Food: Rodents, small birds and mammals, lizards, frogs, insects.

Similar species: African Grass Owl is dark brown above.

Pied Kingfisher

Ceryle rudis

African names:
Bontvisvanger (A);
isaxwila (X);
isiquba (Z).

Average size: Length 25-29 cm;
wing 13-15 cm.

Identification: Distinctive
black-and-white coloration.
Black bill, legs and feet.
Male has double breast band;
female has single, incomplete
breast band.

Call: High-pitched, rattling
twitters and squeaks.

Where found: Virtually throughout, on open water (rivers, lakes,
dams, estuaries, coastal waters).

Habits: Usually in pairs or family
groups. Hunts from perch or by
hovering over water; beats prey
on perch before swallowing.

Nesting: In spring and summer.
Nests in burrow in sandbank,
sometimes in small colonies.

Lays two to six eggs. Incubation[G]
period probably about two weeks.

Notes: Sometimes breeds
cooperatively, with young of
previous brood helping to rear
the new chicks.

Status: Common resident.

Food: Mostly fish, some
crustaceans and insects.

Similar species: Giant Kingfisher
is much larger with rufous[G] breast.

African Hoopoe

Upupa africana

African names: Afrikaanse Hoephoep (A); ubhobhoyi (X); uziningweni (Z).

Average size: Length 25-28 cm; wing 13-15 cm.

Identification: Dove-sized. Orange-brown head, back and underparts; black-tipped crest; boldly black-and-white-barred wings; black tail with white base. Long, thin, bill curves slightly downward. Short legs.

Call: 'Hoop-hoop-hoop'.

Where found: Throughout, in woodland, gardens, parks, thornveld.

Habits: Usually solitary[G] or in pairs. Probes ground with bill looking for food. Raises crest on alighting or when alarmed.

Nesting: Spring and summer. Nests in existing hole; rears up to three broods per season. Lays up to

six eggs, which hatch after about three weeks. Female incubates[G].

Notes: Its nest becomes very dirty and smelly, probably deterring predators.

Status: Common resident.

Food: Insects, earthworms, small snakes, frogs, termites, lizards.

Similar species: None.

Crested Barbet

Trachyphonus vaillantii

African name: Kuifkophout-kapper (A).

Average size: Length 23 cm; wing 9-11 cm.

Identification: Yellow face and underparts, streaked red; small black crest and black breastband. Upperparts blackish, scalloped white; rump red.

Call: Penetrating trilling by male; answering 'puka-puka' by female.

Where found: In northern and eastern regions in woodland, forest, dry savannah, parks, gardens.

Habits: Common in suburban gardens.

Nesting: Breeds throughout year, mainly in spring and summer; may rear up to four broods per season. Both sexes dig nest holes, in which two to four white eggs are laid. These hatch after about two weeks.

Both male and female incubate[G] eggs and feed chicks.

Notes: Territorial[G]; does not tolerate other bird species.

Food: Mainly insects (termites); also fruit, snails and birds' eggs.

Similar species: Yellowheaded form of Blackcollared Barbet has a black bill, olive back, rump and wings, and lacks crest.

Fork-tailed Drongo

Dicrurus adsimilis

African names: Mikstertbyvanger (A); intengu (X, Z).

Average size: Length 23-25 cm; wing 13-14 cm.

Identification: Longish, deeply notched tail. Red eyes.

Call: Loud, jumbly, discordant song; also imitates other birds, including Pearlspotted Owl.

Where found: Avoids forest interiors and open habitats.

Habits: Bold and aggressive. Flies out from perch to catch prey; returns to perch to eat its catch.

Nesting: Mainly in summer; may raise two or three broods per season. Lays two to four eggs, which hatch after about three weeks.

Notes: Occasionally plunge-dives to catch fish.

Status: Common resident.

Food: Insects (bees), small birds, fish, lizards.

Similar species: Squaretailed Drongo and Southern Black Flycatcher are smaller, and their tails are only slightly notched; latter has black eyes.

Pied Crow

Corvus albus

African names: Witborskraai (A); igwangwa (X); igwababa (Z).

Average size: Length 46-52 cm; wing 33-39 cm.

Identification: Shiny black, with white breast and broad white collar around neck.

Call: Harsh, deep, loud 'kraaa'.

Where found: Virtually throughout.

Habits: Scavenger. Frequents rubbish dumps; forages on ground. Also catches small birds in flight.

Nesting: Mainly in spring and summer. Builds large nest in tall tree or on telephone pole. Lays up to seven eggs, which hatch after about three weeks.

Notes: Intelligent and cocky, struts about with arrogant confidence. Sometimes harasses large birds of prey at carcasses.

Status: Common resident.

Food: Seeds, fruit, frogs, reptiles, fish, birds, eggs, small mammals, ectoparasites (on game mammals), carrion (usually road kills).

Similar species: Whitenecked Raven lacks white breast and has shorter tail and larger head. House Crow is smaller, with grey breast and collar.

Dark-capped Bulbul

Pycnonotus tricolor

African names: Swartoogtiptol (A); ikhwebula (X); iphothwe (Z).

Average size: Length 20-22 cm; wing 10 cm.

Identification: Smallish. Slightly crested, black head. Dark eye ring. Greyish-brown back; dark brown breast, whitish belly, lemon-yellow undertail.

Call: Lively, liquid notes.

Where found: In north and east, in wide variety of habitats; woodland, forest edge, plantations, gardens.

Habits: Usually in pairs. Very vocal and conspicuous, often calls from top of trees.

Nesting: Year round, mainly in spring and summer. Cup of dry grass and twigs built in tree. Two or three eggs are laid, which hatch after about two weeks.

Female incubates[G]; male feeds her while she is on the nest.

Notes: Mobs and scolds owls, hawks and snakes. Sometimes known as 'Toppies'. Parasitised[G] by Jacobin Cuckoo.

Status: Abundant resident.

Food: Fruit, nectar, insects, lizards.

Similar species: Cape Bulbul has white eye wattle; African Redeyed Bulbul has red eye wattle; Terrestrial Bulbul has white throat.

Olive Thrush

Turdus olivaceus

African names:
Olyflyster (A);
umswi (X);
umunswi (Z).

Average size: Length 24 cm;
wing 13 cm.

Identification: Dark olive-brown above. Grizzled white throat. Dull orange underparts, washed olive at sides.

Call: Thin 'tseep' alarm and take-off call; fluty, trilling song.

Where found: Montane forests, parks, gardens and plantations. Confined largely to South Africa.

Habits: Usually singly or in pairs. Forages energetically on ground, scratching in fallen leaves and debris. Begins singing every morning before dawn.

Nesting: Year round, mostly in spring and summer. Nest is large bowl built in tree. Up to four eggs are laid. These are incubated^G by female and hatch after two weeks. Both sexes feed young.

Notes: Although shy in forest habitats, this bird is bolder in suburban gardens.

Status: Common resident.

Food: Insects, molluscs, spiders, small lizards, fruit, seeds.

Similar species: Kurrichane Thrush is smaller, and has an orange eye ring and black malar stripes. Orange Ground Thrush shows white bars on folded wings.

Cape Robin-Chat

Cossypha caffra

African names: Gewone Janfrederik (A); ugaga (X); umbhekle (Z).

Average size: Length 16-18 cm; wing 8-9 cm.

Identification: Black face with white eyebrow. Light orange throat and breast. Grey belly. Orange tail with black centre.

Call: Melodious whistling; often sings before dawn.

Where found: South Africa, southern Namibia and eastern Zimbabwe, in forest edge, montane scrub, fynbos, gardens, parks and farmlands.

Habits: Usually solitary[G] or in pairs. Keeps mostly to dense undergrowth; sings from perch.

Nesting: Regionally variable. Male builds nest on ground or in hole, in which up to four eggs are laid. These hatch after about two weeks. Female incubates[G]; both sexes feed young.

Notes: Parasitised[G] by Redchested Cuckoo; as soon as cuckoo hatches, it evicts robin's own young from nest.

Status: Common resident.

Food: Insects, spiders, worms, small frogs, lizards, fruit.

Similar species: Chorister and Heuglin's robins are wholly orange below; Whitethroated Robin has white throat and breast.

Cape Wagtail

Motacilla capensis

African names: Gewone Kwikkie (A); umcelu (X); umvemve (Z).

Average size: Length 18-20 cm; wing 8 cm.

Identification: Dull greyish-brown above; dull off-white below. Narrow, slate-grey breastband. Creamy-white eyebrow.

Call: Clear, piping 'tseep'; whistled, trilling song.

Where found: Near water, parks and gardens.

Habits: Usually solitary^G or in pairs. Gregarious^G when not breeding. Forages energetically on ground. Wags tail up and down.

Nesting: Year round, mainly in spring and summer; may raise up to four broods per season. Builds bulky nest, well concealed, in which up to seven putty-coloured eggs are laid; these hatch after about two weeks. Both parents incubate^G and feed young.

Notes: A rather dull bird compared with other wagtails of the region.

Status: Common resident.

Food: Insects, small fish, tadpoles, food scraps.

Similar species: African Pied Wagtail is strikingly black and white; Longtailed Wagtail has longer tail, white underparts and clearer grey underparts.

Common Fiscal

Lanius collaris

African names: Gewone Fiskaal-laksman (A); inxanxadi (X); iqola (Z).

Average size: Length 21-23 cm; wing 9-10 cm.

Identification: Black above, white below; at rest shows bold white 'V' on back. Longish, white-edged tail. Heavy, hooked bill.

Call: Piping and grating notes; also imitates other birds.

Where found: Virtually throughout, except in forest and desert.

Habits: Territorial[G]. Perches conspicuously. May be very aggressive towards other birds.

Nesting: Year round; may raise several broods per season. Female builds thick-walled bowl in tree, in which up to five eggs are laid; these hatch after about two weeks. Both sexes feed chicks.

Notes: Often seen in gardens, where it chases off other bird species. Known as 'Jackie Hangman' for its habit of impaling uneaten prey on thorns or spikes.

Status: Common resident.

Food: Insects, small lizards, frogs and birds.

Similar species: Fiscal Flycatcher has a slimmer bill and a shorter tail with conspicuous white side patches.

Fiscal Flycatcher

Sigelus silens

African names: Fiskaalvlieëvanger (A); icola (X).

Average size: Length 17-20 cm; wing 9-10 cm.

Identification: Male black above, female dark brown above. White below. Bold white wing stripe. Black tail with large, rectangular white windows. Slender bill.

Call: Weak, chattering song.

Where found: Virtually throughout South Africa, in thornveld, bush and scrub, exotic plantations and suburban gardens.

Habits: Usually singly or in pairs. Bold and conspicuous. Sometimes catches insects in flight.

Nesting: Spring and summer. Nest is lined, shallow bowl of twigs, built in fork of tree. Two to four finely speckled, pale greenish-blue eggs are laid; these hatch after about two weeks.

Notes: Similar to the far more aggressive Common Fiscal Shrike. Has been seen eating porridge from dog's bowls.

Status: Common resident; endemic[G].

Food: Insects, fruit, aloe nectar.

Similar species: Common Fiscal Shrike has longer tail, and stout, hooked bill.

Red-winged Starling

Onychognathus morio

African names: Rooivlerkspreeu (A); isomi (X); insomi (Z).

Average size: Length 27-29 cm; wing 14-16 cm.

Identification: Large, elegant bird with dark eyes, short legs and long tail. Male glossy blue-black; female has a grey head. Rich chestnut flight feathers.

Call: Mellow, whistling song.

Where found: In mountainous areas in south and east; also in Okavango Delta.

Habits: Gregarious[G]; in pairs when breeding. Moves with bounding hops. Bold and conspicuous; highly aggressive near nest, 'divebombing' intruders.

Nesting: In spring and summer. Nest is bowl in which two to four eggs are laid; these hatch after two to three weeks. Female incubates[G]; both sexes feed young.

Notes: One of the most familiar starlings, readily adapted to city-centre living; frequently nests on buildings. Probes for ticks on the backs of cows.

Status: Common resident.

Food: Fruit, insects, ticks, millipedes, lizards, aloe nectar.

Similar species: Palewinged Starling has a pale eye and whitish flight feathers.

Cape Glossy Starling

Lamprotornis nitens

African names: Kleinglansspreeu (A); inyakrini (X); ikhwezi (Z).

Average size: Length 22-25 cm; wing 12-15 cm.

Identification: Iridescent blue-green, washed faintly greenish on ear coverts. Green belly and flanks. Bright orange-yellow eye.

Call: Distinctive, two-syllabled, 'turr-rree' callnote on take-off; pleasant, jumbled warblings.

Where found: Virtually throughout; in savannah, bush, scrub, mixed woodland, urban areas.

Habits: In pairs when breeding, otherwise gregarious[G]; gathers in small flocks. Runs well.

Nesting: Mainly in spring and summer; rarely into winter. Nest a pad in natural hole or under eaves in which two to four lightly speckled, light greenish-blue eggs are laid. Both sexes feed young, sometimes helped by young from previous broods.

Notes: Very similar to the blue-eared starlings.

Status: Common, widespread resident.

Food: Omnivorous.

Similar species: Greater Blue-eared Starling and Southern Lesser Blue-eared Starling have dark blue and magenta bellies, respectively. Both have full ear patches.

Amethyst Sunbird

Chalcomitra amethystina

African names:
Afrikaanse Swart-
suikerbekkie (A);
ingcungcu (X).

Average size: Length 15 cm;
wing 6-8 cm.

Identification: Male mostly
sooty-black, with bright
metallic-green forehead and
metallic-purple throat and
rump. Female grey above, tinged
olive, and creamy-white below;
streaked blackish on throat and
breast. Long, black bill curves
downwards.

Call: Fast twittering and chattering.

Where found: Forest edge,
woodland, savannah, parks
and gardens.

Habits: Usually solitary[G] or in
pairs. Restless and aggressive.
Often hovers when feeding.

Nesting: Varies regionally. Nest
with side-top entrance, built by
female, suspended from branch or
built on wires or light fittings
around houses. Up to three eggs
are laid, which hatch after about
two weeks. Female incubates[G] and
feeds young.

Notes: Occasionally parasitised[G]
by Klaas's Cuckoo.

Status: Common resident.

Food: Nectar, insects and spiders.

Similar species: Scarletchested
Sunbird has large scarlet breast
patch. Dusky Sunbird is smaller
and has a white belly.

House Sparrow

Passer domesticus

African names: Huismossie (A).

Average size: Length 14 cm; wing 7 cm.

Identification: Brown above, with grey rump. Male has grey cap, reddish-brown back, white cheeks and black throat. Female is duller grey-brown and has off-white eye stripe.

Call: Sharp, harsh, penetrating chirps and cheeps.

Where found: Throughout, always around human habitation.

Habits: In pairs or family groups when breeding, otherwise gregarious^G, sometimes in flocks of hundreds. Hops about on ground; sometimes hawks flying insects.

Nesting: Year round, mainly in spring and summer. Nest is untidy. Lays two to five eggs which hatch after about two weeks. Both sexes incubate^G and feed young.

Notes: Most cosmopolitan bird in the world. Introduced in Durban in late 1800s and spread quickly, reaching northern areas of region by the 1960s.

Status: Common to abundant resident.

Food: Seeds, buds, fruit, insects, spiders, household scraps.

Similar species: Male Cape Sparrow has black face and cap; Great Sparrow is more rufous^G above and has chestnut rump.

Southern Red Bishop

Euplectes orix

African names: Suidelike Rooivink (A); umlilo (X); ibomvana (Z).

Average size: Length 13 cm; wing 6-8 cm.

Identification: Breeding male has black breast, forehead, face, and throat; rest of head, upperparts and breastband brilliant orange-scarlet; brown wings and tail. Female and non-breeding male are boldly streaked buff and dark brown above; buffy eyebrow; dark brown wings and tail.

Call: Sharp 'chiz-chiz' call notes; wheezy, whiny song.

Where found: Virtually throughout, except in arid and mountainous regions; on wetland fringes, gardens, fields and open grassland.

Habits: Gregarious^G; forms dense colonies in reedbeds.

Nesting: In spring and summer, polygamous^G male puffs out breast and displays^G with bee-like flight. Male weaves nest, female lines it. Lays two to five eggs, which hatch in less than two weeks.

Notes: Nests often parasitised^G by Diederick Cuckoo.

Status: Common, widespread resident.

Food: Seeds, insects.

Similar species: Firecrowned Bishop breeding male has scarlet forecrown and black wings and tail.

Southern Masked Weaver

Ploceus velatus

African names:
Swartkeelgeelvink
(A); ihobohobo (X);
ihlokohloko (Z).

Average size: Length 14-16 cm;
wing 7-9 cm.

Identification: Breeding male has
black mask ending in point on
upper breast; yellow hind crown
and nape; red eye. Female lacks
mask and is light olive-brownish
above; whitish belly; brown eye.

Call: Harsh swizzling; sharp 'chik'
alarm note.

Where found: Virtually throughout; favours open habitats.

Habits: Gregarious[G], often
breeding in large colonies.
Displays[G] by hanging under nest,
fanning wings and swizzling.

Nesting: In winter, spring and
summer; polygamous[G] male may
have up to eight broods a season.
Nest is neat. Female lays two to
four eggs, which are incubated[G] by
her and hatch after about two
weeks. Female feeds young.

Notes: The casanovas of the bird
world: males have up to 12 nests.

Status: Common resident.

Food: Insects, seeds, flower
parts, nectar.

Similar species: Spottedbacked
Weaver has heavily spotted back;
Lesser Masked Weaver has white
eyes and grey legs.

Cape White-eye

Zosterops capensis

African names: Kaapse Glasogie (A); intukwane (X); umehlwane (Z).

Average size: Length 12 cm; wing 7 cm.

Identification: Greyish-green above. Yellow throat and undertail. White eye-ring. Short bill. Some regional variation in colour.

Call: Long, jerky, reedy song; sweet, piping, trilled callnotes.

Where found: Throughout South Africa and in most parts of Namibia, in forest, woodland, savannah, parks and gardens, riverine scrub and bush.

Habits: In pairs when breeding; otherwise gregarious[G]. Drinks and bathes frequently. Forages restlessly in undergrowth.

Nesting: In spring and summer, sometimes winter. Nest is a small, neat, thin-walled cup, in which two to four eggs are laid. Both sexes incubate[G] eggs, which hatch in less than two weeks. Both sexes feed young.

Notes: One of the best-known garden birds of the region. Although considered a pest by some fruit-growers, they do also eat aphids and insects that are harmful to fruit.

Status: Common resident; endemic[G].

Food: Insects, spiders, nectar and fruit.

Similar species: Yellow White-eye is yellower above and has uniform, bright yellow underparts.

Cape Canary

Serinus canicollis

African names: Kaapse Kanarie (A); umlonji (X); umzwilili (Z).

Average size: Length 13 cm; wing 7 cm.

Identification: Slender. Greenish-gold crown and face; rest of head blue-grey. Light olive, finely streaked back; dull yellow rump and yellow below. Longish, notched, olive tail with yellow margins.

Call: Very sweet, loud, clear trills and twitters.

Where found: In south and east; favours mountainous habitats; also fynbos, grassland, gardens and parks.

Habits: Gregarious[G]. In pairs or small family groups when breeding; otherwise in flocks, sometimes numbering hundreds.

Nesting: Mainly in spring and summer, depending on locality. Female builds thick-walled cup in tree, in which two to five variably coloured eggs are laid; these hatch after about two weeks. Female incubates[G]; both sexes feed young.

Status: Common resident.

Food: Seeds, fruit, flowers.

Similar species: Yelloweyed Canary has bolder, diagnostic[G] facial markings; Forest Canary is heavily streaked below and is darker above.

Glossary

Colonial: Associating in close proximity when nesting.

Diagnostic: Conclusively identifying a given bird (a bird that has a 'diagnostic' feature can be identified by that feature).

Display: Ritualised behaviour of a bird that wishes to attract a mate or defend a territory.

Endemic: A species whose breeding and non-breeding ranges are confined to one region (a species that breeds only in one region but moves away at other times is called a 'breeding endemic').

Gregarious: Living together in flocks.

Guano: The excrement of fish-eating seabirds, highly valued as fertilizer.

Host: A bird that incubates and rears another species' young (see 'Parasite').

Hybridise: Interbreed.

Immature: Not yet adult.

Incubate: To regulate egg temperature with the body.

Monogamous: Having only one mate during a breeding season.

Parasite (brood parasite): A bird that lays its eggs in other birds' nests (see 'Host'). Chicks are reared by the host.

Polygamous: Having more than one mate during a breeding season.

Roost: The place where birds rest or sleep.

Rufous: Reddish brown.

Solitary: Not living in organised colonies or large groups ('in pairs' means two birds are found together).

Stoop: Swoop down.

Territory: An area that a bird establishes and then defends against others; birds that defend a territory are called 'territorial'.